Activities for Home Visits

Partnering With
Preschool Families

Activities for Home Visits

Partnering With Preschool Families

Suzanne Gainsley and Julie Hoelscher

HIGHSCOPE
PRESS ®

Ypsilanti, Michigan

Published by
HighScope® Press
A division of the
HighScope Educational Research Foundation
600 North River Street
Ypsilanti, Michigan 48198-2898
734.485.2000, FAX 734.485.0704
Orders: 800.40.PRESS; Fax: 800.442.4FAX; www.highscope.org
E-mail: *press@highscope.org*

Editors: Jennifer Burd, Marcella Fecteau Weiner
Cover design, text design, production: Judy Seling
Illustrations: Jane DeLancey, Judy Seling (p. 34), Noah Weiner (p. 67)
Photography:
Bob Foran: pp. 12, 26, 39
Gregory Fox: pp. 22, 29, 48, 65
HighScope Staff: pp. 2, 6, 16, 25, 31, 37, 58, 61, 69, 71 back cover
Peter de Ruiter: p. 40

Library of Congress Cataloging-in-Publication Data

Gainsley, Suzanne, 1964-

Activities for home visits : partnering with preschool families / Suzanne Gainsley and Julie Hoelscher.

p. cm.

ISBN 978-1-57379-456-5 (soft cover : alk. paper) 1. Education, Preschool--Activity programs. 2. Home visits (Education) 3. Education, Preschool--Parent participation. I. Hoelscher, Julie, 1949- II. Title.

LB1140.35.C74G345 2010

371.19'2--dc22

2009043287

Printed in the United States of America
10 9 8 7 6 5 4 3 2

Contents

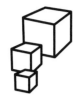

Mathematics 41

Science and Technology 51

Social Studies 59

The Arts 63

Acknowledgments

We are appreciative for the opportunity to collaborate and learn from each other. We would like to acknowledge Marcella Weiner, our editor, whose keen eye for details makes this a better publication. We would also like to thank Beth Marshall, who initiated this project, and Ann Epstein, to whom we rely on for writing support. Finally, thanks go to Shannon Lockhart, Polly Neill, Kay Rush, and Emily Thompson, our colleagues in the Early Childhood Department who are always available to offer good counsel, resources, and an optimistic vision.

Thoughts About Home Visiting

Parents have the privilege of being their child's first and most influential teachers. While many parents feel comfortable and confident with this role, they also may want and welcome support and guidance.

Think about the kinds of educational goals or expectations your parents have for their young children. Typical goals may include their children learning numbers and letters of the alphabet, developing friendships, thinking independently, and enjoying school. Although parents may know what their goals and expectations are, they may be unsure of how to help their children accomplish them. One of the primary goals of home visits, therefore, is to build relationships with parents and families so they have the knowledge and the skills to help them with their very important role in their children's learning.

Current research supports the value of these home visits. According to the Harvard Family Research Project (Weiss, Caspe, & Lopez, 2006), teachers can improve child learning outcomes by (1) establishing strong formal and informal home-school relationships and (2) helping parents take responsibility for their children's learning by emphasizing activities in the home and community that promote learning. Many early childhood education programs have therefore required teachers to make regular home visits to the families they serve. Although the required number of visits may vary by program, home visits, in combination with other parent involvement activities, can lead to positive outcomes for child learning.

1

The purpose of this book is to help you, the early childhood educator, conduct successful home visits that build partnerships with parents and families to support every child's early school achievement.

Getting the Most Out of Home Visits

Making Families Comfortable

Initial home visits often occur at the beginning of the school year or upon enrollment of new children, where you meet and learn about the children and families in the family's home, a more comfortable and less intimidating setting for children and parents than an unfamiliar classroom. Most children are excited about having you visit their home. Generally, children will show you their beds, their pets, or their favorite toys. During the initial home visit, you have the opportunity to observe family culture, talk to families about their interests and the interests and/or needs of their children, and get a firsthand look at children on their own turf. You can use this information to provide classroom materials and activities that are reflective of a family's culture, values, and practices.

Home visits help teachers build relationships with parents and families.

While some families may be comfortable with the idea of home visits, others may be reluctant to schedule visits for a variety of reasons. It is important to explain the purpose of home visits to parents before you visit to lessen parents' apprehension.

Commonly, parents may fear that they will be judged on their home environment or parenting skills. If this is the case, reassure parents that you are not visiting to check up on them but rather to introduce yourself, meet the family, and help their child make a smooth transition to school. If parents are still hesitant, suggest that your initial visit be in a neutral location, such as the public library, park, or playground. Later, once trust is established, parents may feel more comfortable inviting you to their home.

Significant language barriers between home and school may also make parents reluctant to schedule home visits and reduce their general involvement in the classroom. Greeting parents in their home language (if possible) and showing genuine interest in their culture during home visits will help bridge this language divide. Have parents name classroom materials in their home language and share common expressions that you might use with their child during your classroom's routine.

Other barriers to parental involvement in home visits may include parents' bad memories about school, their lack of school success, or mistrust or hostility toward schools in general. Using the communication tips (see the sidebar below) may help ease some of that tension.

Establishing a Routine

It is important to establish a regular routine for conducting home visits so that parents and children know what to expect. At the time of preschool enrollment, talk with the family about why you conduct home visits. For example, you might tell the family that home visits are conducted to discuss some shared goals for the child, to help the teacher understand the family's culture, to establish trust, and to build connections between home and school. Explain that you will strengthen these connections later on when the child is in school, by telling the child stories about the home visit and sharing the pictures you are taking of what happens.

At the beginning of the year provide a sign-up sheet for the next scheduled home visit. Be sure that the home visit is held at a convenient time for families, and let them know that you will be bringing materials to the visit for the whole family to

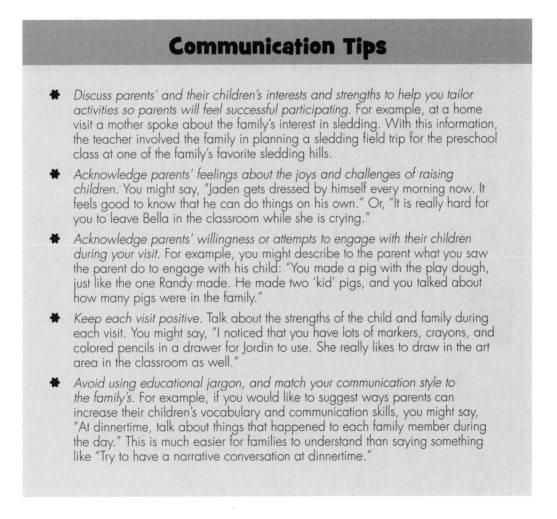

Communication Tips

* *Discuss parents' and their children's interests and strengths to help you tailor activities so parents will feel successful participating.* For example, at a home visit a mother spoke about the family's interest in sledding. With this information, the teacher involved the family in planning a sledding field trip for the preschool class at one of the family's favorite sledding hills.

* *Acknowledge parents' feelings about the joys and challenges of raising children.* You might say, "Jaden gets dressed by himself every morning now. It feels good to know that he can do things on his own." Or, "It is really hard for you to leave Bella in the classroom while she is crying."

* *Acknowledge parents' willingness or attempts to engage with their children during your visit.* For example, you might describe to the parent what you saw the parent do to engage with his child: "You made a pig with the play dough, just like the one Randy made. He made two 'kid' pigs, and you talked about how many pigs were in the family."

* *Keep each visit positive.* Talk about the strengths of the child and family during each visit. You might say, "I noticed that you have lots of markers, crayons, and colored pencils in a drawer for Jordin to use. She really likes to draw in the art area in the classroom as well."

* *Avoid using educational jargon, and match your communication style to the family's.* For example, if you would like to suggest ways parents can increase their children's vocabulary and communication skills, you might say, "At dinnertime, talk about things that happened to each family member during the day." This is much easier for families to understand than saying something like "Try to have a narrative conversation at dinnertime."

use. Establish at the beginning your expectation that parents will participate in the activity that you have prepared.

Following Up

At the home visit, keep in mind what you will do to follow up later with parents and children. For example, you might ask the family what pictures they would like you to take of them for display in the classroom. After the home visit, send a thank-you note that includes an anecdote of something that happened. You might also extend the home visit into the classroom by providing a shared story, fingerplay, or song that you create with the child that you visited. This provides an opportunity for a storytelling experience important for a child's reading and writing success later on (Keyser, 2006). Finally, many of the activities in this book can be used on subsequent home visits so that the family members can see how the child has developed.

Using the Activities

This book introduces activities that you can do during regularly scheduled home visits. The activities provide opportunities for you to share knowledge about child development, model positive adult-child interaction strategies, and introduce parents and children to developmentally appropriate activities to do at home. Children learn about healthy relationships by observing parents and teachers communicate respectfully as equal partners.

Each activity in this book focuses on one of eight curriculum content areas:

 Approaches to Learning

 Language, Literacy, and Communication

 Social and Emotional Development

 Physical Development, Health, and Well-Being

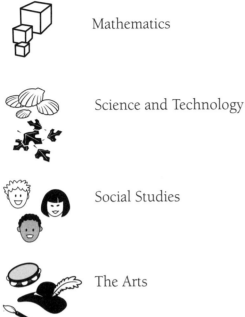

Mathematics

Science and Technology

Social Studies

The Arts

Each activity contains the following elements:

- **Activity Title and Content Area Icon:** At the beginning of each activity, you will see an icon (see above) representing the primary content area the activity supports.

- **Content Areas:** This part lists one or more of the eight curriculum content areas that this activity supports. If the activity involves several content areas, the primary content area is listed first.

- **Family Messages:** This section describes the descriptions for curriculum content areas in simple terms. You can share this information with parents to help them relate their children's play to learning outcomes.

- **Materials:** The materials needed for each activity are usually available in most early childhood classrooms or are simple to make. Once familiar with how the activities support active learning in each content area, you may find it easy to substitute alternative classroom materials and activities.

> During **active learning** children construct knowledge through their direct experiences with people, materials, and ideas.

- **Beginning, Middle, End,** and **Home Extensions:** Activities are outlined with a beginning, middle, ending, and home extensions and are based on the principles of **active learning.**

Before using one of these activities during your home visit, be sure to read through the activity several times and make sure you have all the necessary materials.

Modeling Adult-Child Interaction Strategies

Keep in mind the following interaction strategies to model for parents during each activity:

- *Sit on the same level as the child.* If the child is on the floor, invite parents to join you on the floor.

- *Imitate what child is doing; that is, play with the same materials in the same way as the child.* For example, during one home visit, Emma took her portion of play dough that had marbles hidden inside. She squeezed the dough with both hands. The teacher also squeezed the dough with both hands.

- *Make observations and comments about what you see the child doing.* While watching Emma squeeze the play dough with the marbles hidden inside, the teacher commented, "It looks like you have lots of marbles in your dough." Emma responded, "Yeah, and I am going to pick them out and line 'em up."

Being on the same level as the child during a home visit models for parents an adult-child interaction strategy used in the classroom.

- *Ask open-ended questions, but ask them sparingly.* Open-ended questions encourage children to talk more, because these types of questions cannot be answered by a simple "yes" or "no." For example, at Nathan's home, the teacher laid out the puzzle pieces and asked Nathan, "What do you think this puzzle picture might be?" Nathan responded, "I think it's a bear because...look...it's furry." Rather than asking more questions about why Nathan thought it looked furry, the teacher waited until he completed the puzzle and commented, "It looks like you were right; it is a big, grizzly bear." Questions can help get a conversation going, but it is more important not to inundate a child with questions so that he or she feels overwhelmed.

- *Follow the child's pace and interests.* During one home visit, Belinda was measuring the number of giant steps to the garage. She then turned around at the garage door and decided to make "tiptoe" steps to the sidewalk. The teacher followed Belinda by making tiptoe steps to the sidewalk (Epstein, 2007).

⁂

We hope that you will use these activities to help build a strong teacher-parent partner relationship that not only focuses on open communication and respect for diversity but also provides parents with developmental information and support for their role as their child's most influential teachers.

References

Epstein, A. S. (2007). *Essentials of active learning in preschool: Getting to know the HighScope Curriculum.* Ypsilanti, MI: HighScope Press.

Keyser, J. (2006). *From parents to partners: Building a family-centered early childhood program.* St. Paul, MN: Readleaf Press.

Weiss, H., Caspe, M., & Lopez, E. M. (2006). *Family involvement in early childhood education* (Family Involvement Makes a Difference No. 1). Cambridge, MA: Harvard Family Research Project.

Approaches to Learning

CONTENT AREAS
Approaches to Learning

MATERIALS
- 5 large index cards
- Markers

1   Helping at Home

Family Messages:

- Young children are often interested in copying the actions of adults and may sometimes ask to help with household tasks.

- When thinking about giving your child a household chore to complete, consider his interests. Allow your child to talk about his plan for helping, and then give him the opportunity to follow through.

Beginning:

- With the child and family, make a heading on each of the index cards of an area in the house where the child could accomplish a household task. You could have headings such as *Laundry, Kitchen, Outside,* and *Bedroom.*

- Under each heading, write down the child's ideas and the family's ideas for tasks the child could complete. Under the kitchen heading, for example, you might write down "Setting the table," "Wiping a counter," or "Putting away silverware."

Middle:

- Let the child choose a task or two from the lists on the cards, and complete the tasks together.

- Talk with the child about what he is doing — remind the family that children need lots of practice to acquire skills!

End:

- End the visit by helping the child and family find a place to post the lists of potential "child tasks."

Home Extensions:

- Ask the family to revisit the lists and perhaps think about other areas where a child could complete a household task.

- Encourage the family to set up a routine in which everyone contributes by doing household chores together (for example, on Saturdays, Nathan takes the sheets off of his bed for laundering).

2 Choosing Balls

Family Messages:

- Children are not accustomed to having decision-making roles. On many occasions, especially in the areas of health and safety, it is necessary for adults to make decisions for children. This activity gives your child an opportunity to have a decision-making role — to make choices about balls and hoops.

- You can show interest in the choices your child makes by commenting on her ideas, imitating her actions, and letting her be the decision maker.

Beginning:

- Lay out the balls outside, and let the child experiment with the balls. Set the hoops behind you.

- Comment on what the child does with the balls, and imitate her actions. For example, you might say, "I see that the ball you are using bounces. I am going to see if this other ball bounces too."

Middle:

- Introduce the hoops by putting them in front of you on the ground. Ask "How might you use these hoops with the balls?"

- Follow the child's lead, and imitate what she is doing with the balls and hoops. Play as a partner by joining the child's game, if invited.

- Describe what the child is doing with the balls and hoops, and then describe what you are doing with them. You might say, "I see you bouncing the ball inside the hoop. I'm trying to bounce the ball inside and then outside the hoop."

End:

- Ask the child what she enjoyed doing most with the balls and hoops.

- Have the child help you put away the balls and hoops.

CONTENT AREAS
Approaches to Learning

Physical Development, Health, and Well-Being

MATERIALS
- Variety of balls
- 2 Hula-Hoops

Home Extensions:

- Ask the family if they have any balls and hoops to use at home. If not, help them come up with materials they could substitute for balls and hoops (balls can be made from crumpled paper and tape; any container, such as a basket, could take the place of a hoop; rope could be used to make an enclosure in which to throw a ball).

Encourage parents to look around their house and yard for items that can be used as balls and hoops — an old tire can make a perfect hoop!

3   Planting Flowers

Family Messages:

- Your young child is developing a sense of community. As part of the community at home, at school, and in the neighborhood community in which we each live, children are asked to take on responsibilities for the well-being of the community.

- Today we are asking your child to choose flower seeds to plant and water and transplant in your yard or flower box when the plant is strong enough. Taking care of plants sends your child a message about his importance in shared community responsibilities.

Beginning:

- Talk with the child about flowering plants. You might ask, "Are there any in the yard?" or "Have you watched anyone plant flower seeds?"

- Let the child choose which seeds he would like to plant in the cups.

Middle:

- Let the child put soil in the cup and plant the seeds. Use a paper cup for watering.

- Show the child the watering and growth chart. Let him draw what the cups and their contents look like today.

End:

- With the family, help the child find a place to put the cups where they will get sunlight.

- Find a place to display the watering and growth chart.

Home Extensions:

- Encourage families to discuss the plants' growth. Have the family help the child record the plants' growth with a ruler and write the measurement in the box on the graph.

- Let family members know that they should help the child find a permanent spot outside for the flowering plants.

CONTENT AREAS
Approaches to Learning
Social Studies

MATERIALS
- 4 paper cups
- 3 kinds of seeds
- Potting soil
- Ruler
- Weekly plant watering and growth chart (see p. 14) to keep track of watering and to notice changes in the plant as it grows

Weekly Plant Watering and Growth Chart

Name _____

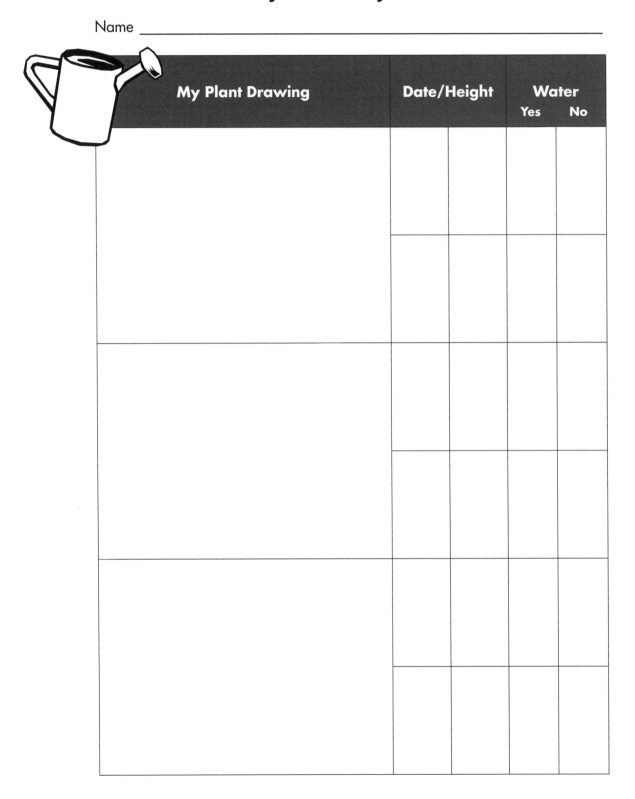

My Plant Drawing	Date/Height		Water	
			Yes	No

4   Classroom Routine Booklet

Family Messages:

- Classroom routines help meet young children's need for consistency and predictability. They also help children anticipate what is next and transition from one activity to the next.

- This booklet of the classroom routine matches the symbols of the events that occur in the preschool class every day.

Beginning:

- Give the child a copy of the classroom routine booklet, and ask her if she knows what the booklet might be about.

Middle:

- Let the child make comments about the classroom routine booklet and follow her lead.

- Ask the child one or two questions about the classroom routine to encourage a discussion about what happens during the day. For example, you might ask one of these questions:

    1. What do you like to do during work (or choice) time?

    2. What do you like to do during outside time?

    3. When it is cleanup time, how do you help clean up?

    4. Which parts of the preschool day do you like the most? What is something you do not like to do during preschool?

CONTENT AREAS
Approaches to Learning

Language, Literacy, and Communication

MATERIALS

- Booklet of the classroom routine that matches the classroom routine symbols: use a colored paper for the cover; prepare the classroom routine symbols, one to each sheet of paper in chronological order; staple the booklet together

- Blank booklet for the child and family to create a "family routine" booklet

---

Classroom routine symbols are picture representations that correspond to the different parts of your class routine. For example, you may depict large-group time as a circle of smiley faces, representing the children sitting in a circle. Whatever you decide to use for your classroom routine symbols, make sure that each symbol is meaningful to the children and remains the same for that particular part of the routine. Children's understanding of these symbols helps prepare them for future reading in elementary school.

End:

- After you have completed your conversation using the classroom routine booklet, ask the child where she would like to store it. Tell her that there will also be a classroom routine booklet in the book area in the preschool classroom.

Home Extensions:

- Provide a blank booklet for the child and family to create a family routine booklet. Ask the family to share the booklet with the class. Provide a designated space in the classroom for the family routine booklets.

While sharing the classroom routine booklet, talk to the child about the day's routine. Ask questions, such as "What parts of the day do you like most?"

Language, Literacy, and Communication

CONTENT AREAS
Language, Literacy, and Communication

MATERIALS

- Cloth drawstring bag, paper bag, or basket
- 5 sets of familiar objects with names that rhyme (for example, rocks, socks, and blocks; moons, balloons, and spoons; dogs, frogs, and [Lincoln] logs)

5 Rhyming Objects

Family Messages:

- Rhymes help children hear the sounds that make up words. Specifically, they help children identify and isolate word endings that sound the same.

Beginning:

- Have the child close her eyes while you put one item in the bag and lay the other items in front of you.
- Ask the child to guess what is in the bag. Let her pull the object out of the bag and name it.

Middle:

- Ask the child to look at the other objects in front of you and find ones that rhyme with what was in the bag. If the child is unable to name the rhyming object, model by naming the rhyming objects. For example, you might say, "Let's find objects that rhyme with *rock*. Look…here's a sock and a clock. They rhyme with *rock*."
- Close your eyes, and ask the child to hide an object in the bag from the ones in front of you. Let the child find objects in front of you that rhyme with what she has put in the bag. If the child is unable to find an object that rhymes, model by naming the rhyming objects.
- Take an object that you have brought and help the child find objects in the home that rhyme with that object's name.

End:

- Have the child help you put all of the objects that you brought back in the bag.

Home Extensions:

- Suggest that the family do a scavenger hunt with objects in the home whose names rhyme. For example, they might ask the child, "Can you find something that rhymes with this clock?"

6   Alliteration I Spy

Family Messages:

- This activity builds your child's awareness of initial sounds in words when two or more words in a row begin with the same sound (for example, "tick, tack, toe" or "goodness gracious!"). This repetition of initial sounds is called *alliteration.*

Beginning:

- Read the story with the child, pointing out the common beginning sounds.

Middle:

- Say something like "Let's play a little game with the beginning sounds of words. I spy something in this room that begins with a /d/ sound." If, for example, the child identifies "door," put a piece of tape with the letter *d* on the door. Then you might say, "Can you think of other things in the house that begin with a /d/?" Label the objects with the letter *d.* If the child gives an incorrect answer, say something like "You named the /s/ sound in *sofa.* What other things can you see that start with the /s/ sound?"

- Continue the game with other beginning sounds.

End:

- With the child, remove the tape from the objects that you have labeled.

Home Extensions:

- Suggest that the family play I spy with beginning sounds at mealtimes.

CONTENT AREAS
Language, Literacy, and Communication

MATERIALS
- Storybook that includes alliteration, for example:
  - *The Baby Beebee Bird* by Diane Redfield Massie
  - *The Duchess Bakes a Cake* by Virginia Kahl
  - *Sheep on a Ship* by Nancy Shaw
  - *Silly Sally* by Audrey Wood
- Roll of masking tape
- Marker

CONTENT AREAS
Language, Literacy, and
Communication

MATERIALS

- Collection of
materials that
make noise (for
example, keys on
a ring, cellophane,
newspaper, wooden
blocks, small tins,
chopsticks, an alarm
clock, bells) in a
basket

- Small tape recorder

- Family journal
(small inexpensive
notebook) for writing
down the sounds
child hears on the
neighborhood walk

7   Sounds, Sounds, Sounds

Family Messages:

- Activities like these will encourage your child to hear, locate,
and name environmental sounds. These activities set the
stage for hearing and identifying the subtle sounds that make
up words.

Beginning:

- Ask the child to find out what kinds of noises the objects
make.

Middle:

- Let the child experiment with the materials. Talk with her
about the sounds she hears. Make some sounds with the
objects and comment on the sounds you hear.

- Using a tape recorder, record the sounds that the child makes
with the objects.

- After the child has experimented with the materials, have her
choose her favorite sound.

End:

- Have the child return the materials to the collection basket by identifying the sounds of the objects from the tape
recorder.

Home Extensions:

- Suggest that the parents take a walk through the neighborhood and talk about the sounds they hear. Have them write
down all of the outdoor sounds they heard in the family
journal so the child can share the list with the classroom.

8   Making Connections

Family Messages:

- To understand a story you are telling or reading to them, children need to make connections between what they hear and things they already know. To understand what a story is about, they need to connect the objects, characters, and events in a story to things in their own lives. As a story unfolds, they also need to link the events of the story together. To do this, they have to figure out what goes on in every story event, keep each event in mind, and then connect the series of events into a coherent story.

- This activity helps your child make the connections necessary to understand a story narrative.

CONTENT AREAS
Language, Literacy, and Communication

MATERIALS
- Child's favorite object found in the house

Beginning:

- Have the child describe the object to you. Ask him how he plays with the object.

Middle:

- With the child holding the object, sitting close to you, make up a story about the object that includes three ideas. Think about incorporating the child's known interests, family members, and neighborhood or preschool friends. For example, if the child brings you his favorite car, you might make up this story with three ideas:

Idea # 1: "Jonas got into his red car and decided to drive it to the park."

Idea # 2: "On the way to the park, he saw his mom pushing his sister Kaya in the stroller. They were walking to the park too."

Idea # 3: "When Jonas arrived at the park, he drove until he found his favorite slide. He parked the car near the slide. He jumped out of the car and went right up the steps on the slide and whoosh…down the slide he slid."

End:

- Have the child retell the story about the object, or have the child make up a story about the object.

Home Extensions:

- Encourage the family to look at a photograph album with the child and let him talk about the photos and what he remembers about events. Or, let the child choose a photo in the album to make up a story about.

To understand a story, children need to connect what they are hearing about and looking at to things they know about in their own lives.

9   Animal Cubes

Family Messages:

- Giving your child many opportunities to speak and listen helps to get your child ready to read and write when he goes to school.

- This activity with animal cubes allows your child to make choices and to talk about what he knows.

Beginning:

- Encourage the child to choose pictures to glue onto each side of the cube.

- Help the child cut out and glue the pictures to fit the cube (he may be able to do this by himself).

Middle:

- Tell the child that you are going to take turns rolling the cube and talking about the animals in the pictures.

- Suggest that the child go first. After he rolls the cube, ask him to talk about the animal in the picture. (If the child wants you to go first, give it a try.)

- At your turn, roll the cube and talk about one of the animals.

End:

- When all of the animals have been talked about, give the child the cube to keep for later use with his family members.

Home Extensions:

- Leave an empty cube for the family to create using other pictures that the child enjoys.

CONTENT AREAS
Language, Literacy, and Communication

MATERIALS

- Large cube, which can be made from a half-gallon juice carton (have an extra one, such as a small empty milk carton from school, for Home Extensions)

- Glue

- Scissors

- Old magazines or postcards with pictures of animals

CONTENT AREAS
Language, Literacy, and Communication

MATERIALS
- Objects from a familiar storybook, such as the items found in *Good Night, Gorilla* by Peggy Rathmann
- Familiar storybook the objects are from
- Pillowcase or bag to hold objects

10 Story Bag

Family Messages:

- Retelling a familiar story engages your child in the complex thinking needed to understand a story and re-create it in her mind.

- Retelling also allows your child to enter the lives of story characters and to connect her own experiences to the characters' experiences.

- This activity will help your child retell a story, putting her thoughts into words and letting her try out new words and ideas.

Beginning:

- Read the story to the child, keeping the items in the bag.

Middle:

- After you have finished sharing the story, ask the child to pull out the items in the bag and relate them to where she saw them in the storybook.

- Ask the child which item appeared first, second, third, and so forth.

End:

- Have the child help you put the items back inside the bag.

Home Extensions:

- Ask the parents to find a familiar story that they like to share with their child and choose items that they might find at home to put into a pillowcase. Have the family repeat the activity.

11   Hopscotch With Letter Links

Family Messages:

- Through their experiences with books and print, children recognize that written words are connected to spoken words and carry meaning.

- Children are also beginning to expand upon their letter (alphabetic) knowledge. Your young child is beginning to understand that letters make up words as she reads her own scribbles.

Beginning:

- Let the child choose enough names/pictures that she knows or recognizes to make a hopscotch board.

Middle:

- Set up the hopscotch board with the child, taping down the names/pictures.

- Play hopscotch with the child, calling out the names (or letters, if the child can recognize them) while playing. (*Note:* If the child cannot hop on one foot, encourage her to use both feet.)

End:

- Together, gather the papers used for the hopscotch board to put in an envelope or folder.

Home Extensions:

- Leave copies of all of the names/letter-linked pictures so that the child can play this game at home.

CONTENT AREAS
Language, Literacy, and Communication

MATERIALS

- Letter-linked pictures with names* of child's classmates printed on 8" x 11" sheets of paper (you may want to laminate these)
- Marker (for playing hopscotch)
- Tape
- Envelope or folder

In this example, the child's name is paired with a picture of an automobile, which starts with the same letter and sound as Audrey.

---

*Letter links is a name-learning system that pairs a child's printed name with a picture of a word that starts with the same letter and sound, for example, the name Delia and a picture of a deer. For more information, see *Letter Links: Alphabet Learning With Children's Names* (2003) from HighScope Press or Letter Links Online at www.highscope.org.

CONTENT AREAS
Language, Literacy, and Communication

MATERIALS

* Wordless picture book, for example:
  - *Bears* by Ruth Krauss and Maurice Sendak
  - *A Boy, a Dog, and a Frog* by Mercer Mayer
  - *Changes, Changes* by Pat Hutchins
  - *Flotsam* by David Wiesner
  - *Good Night, Gorilla* by Peggy Rathmann
  - *Tuba Lessons* by T.C. Bartlett
  - *Mama* by Jeanette Winter
  - *Pancakes for Breakfast* by Tomie dePaola
  - *Rainstorm* by Barbara Lehman

12   Wordless Picture Books

Family Messages:

* Children begin their reading journey by reading pictures.

* This activity gives your child an opportunity to tell a story by reading the pictures.

* When reading a picture book to your child, invite conversation by asking a question or making a comment, such as "I wonder what you see on this page." Encourage your child to talk about objects, animals, and people she sees in illustrations on the cover and in the pages of the book.

Beginning:

* Let the child hold and touch the book. Begin by asking the child what she thinks will happen in this book based on what she sees on the cover.

Middle:

* Let the child describe for you what she sees on the pages. Ask her what she thinks will happen next. Converse with the child about things in the pictures she has seen or played with herself.

End:

* Ask the child what she thinks the character might do after the story ends.

Home Extensions:

* Leave the book for the child to read to her family during the week.

Children begin to learn how to read by looking at and "reading" the pictures in the book.

Social and Emotional Development

CONTENT AREAS
Social and Emotional
Development

Social Studies

MATERIALS

- 2 hand mirrors

13   Mirror, Mirror

Family Messages:

- When children are able to express their feelings in words,
  it helps them gain some control over those feelings and the
  actions that accompany them.

- You can help your child recognize emotions by acknowledg-
  ing (naming) and accepting his feelings.

Beginning:

- Give the child a hand mirror, and ask him to make some
  funny faces.

- Hold your own hand mirror, and copy the child's funny face.

- Take turns making funny faces in the mirrors.

Middle:

- Say something like "I wonder what it would look like if you
  had a sad face" to the child.

- Make faces representing other emotions.

- Describe a situation and create a face to represent the cor-
  responding emotion. For example, you might say, "I wonder
  what your face would look like if you got a new puppy."

End:

- Make a sad face in the mirror, and say "Look how I feel now."
  Tell the child that you feel sad because it is time for you to
  leave.

- Ask the child to help you think of happy things (to cheer you
  up) as you put the mirrors away and walk to the door.

Home Extensions:

- Encourage parents to label their emotions and their child's
  emotions throughout the day. For example, they might say,
  "I'm feeling happy that the dishes are washed and I can read
  with you" or "You seem excited that Grandma is coming
  over."

- Encourage parents to talk about or ask about the characters' feelings as they read stories to their child. For example, if a parent is reading a story about Goldilocks and the three bears, he might say, "It looks like Baby Bear is crying. I think he's upset that Goldilocks ate his porridge. How do you think Papa Bear feels?"

Being able to express feelings in words ("Mommy, don't go! I'll miss you!") and having them acknowledged helps make morning transitions a bit easier.

CONTENT AREAS
Social and Emotional
Development

Social Studies

MATERIALS
- Classroom photos of
  children and adults
- Camera

14   Classroom Photos

Family Messages:

- Positive relationships contribute to children's sense of competence and well-being.

- When children feel a part of a group (community), they learn to be open to the personal experiences of others within that group.

Beginning:

- Show the child a photo of himself engaged in an activity at preschool.

- Talk with the child about the photo by describing what you see in the photo. Ask the child open-ended questions about the picture (for example, "What did you do with the blocks after the picture was taken?"), and acknowledge what he says. For example, the child might say, "The road went all the way to the house area." You might respond, "The road stretched all the way to the house area, and then it stopped?"

Middle:

- Say "I have pictures of other children in our class. I wonder what they are doing."

- Encourage the child to have a conversation with you about who are in the pictures, what they are doing, and where they are playing.

- Talk about whether the child enjoys similar activities or has participated in similar experiences.

End:

- Tell the child that you would like to make a classroom photo album with pictures of the children at home.

- Ask the child where he would like to have his picture taken in his home.

Home Extensions:

- Encourage families to look at family photo albums together, and talk about the people and events taking place. Parents can categorize the people in the photos as family members, friends, and neighbors to help child recognize the different types of social groups he belongs to.

In this class, children were encouraged to bring in pictures of special occasions or trips they took to share with the rest of the class.

CONTENT AREAS
Social and Emotional
Development

MATERIALS
- Streamers, ribbon sticks, or scarves
- Instrumental music
- Music player

15   Follow the Leader

Family Messages:

- Being a leader helps a child see herself as a capable person whose ideas are valued by others.

- Children who feel competent have the self-confidence to take on new challenges.

Beginning:

- Tell the child that you have brought materials to use while moving to music.

- Turn on the music, and together explore ways of moving to the music with the materials you have brought.

Middle:

- Copy the way the child is moving, and say "You are the leader. I am following you."

- Take turns being the leader with the child and other family members.

- If the setting permits, take turns leading a parade around the house or yard.

End:

- Have the child lead the parade back to put the materials away.

- Ask the child to choose a way to move to escort you to the door.

Home Extensions:

- Play follow the leader during common transitions at home (for example, as the child hops upstairs to bed, the parent follows the child and hops behind her).

16 Homemade Toothpaste

Family Messages:

- Your child is able to take care of some of her own needs. She should be able to brush her teeth twice each day, with an adult's assistance. It is important for you to model brushing teeth for your child.

- A child is usually able to floss her teeth by 6 or 7 years of age.

- A child's toothbrush should be replaced every 3–4 months.

Beginning:

- Tell the child that she and you are going to make some homemade toothpaste. Ask her if she brushes her teeth with the help of a parent.

- Talk to the child about toothbrushing. Explain that brushing teeth removes plaque. You might say, "Plaque is sticky and soft and comes from the food we eat mixed with germs. We brush our teeth to get rid of plaque, which makes holes in our teeth."

Middle:

- Have the child mix the ingredients according to the rebus recipe.

- Hold the mirror as the child tries out the toothpaste she made.

- Ask her how the toothpaste tastes.

Ending:

- Find a place to keep the homemade paste.

- The child might decide that the paste is too salty. In that case, she may show you the tube of toothpaste that she likes.

Home Extensions:

- Ask the family what other needs their child can handle on her own. Suggest putting laundry or toys away.

CONTENT AREAS

Social and Emotional Development

Science and Technology

Language, Literacy, and Communication

MATERIALS

- Small child's new toothbrush

- Mirror

- Rebus recipe card for the child to read (see p. 34)

- Ingredients for homemade toothpaste (see below)

- Teaspoon

- Small airtight container to keep the paste in

Toothpaste Recipe

4 tsp. baking soda

1 tsp. salt

1 tsp. peppermint extract

Homemade Toothpaste Rebus

Assemble the following:

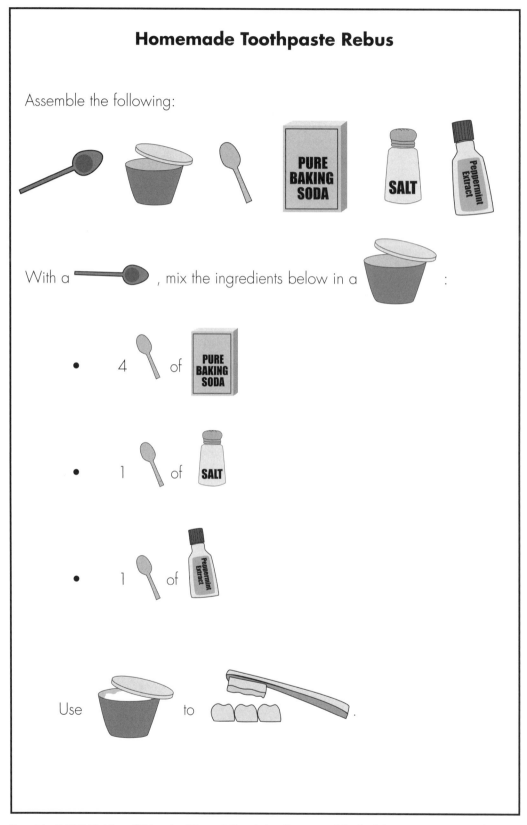

With a ⬤⟍ , mix the ingredients below in a :

- 4 ⟍ of **PURE BAKING SODA**

- 1 ⟍ of **SALT**

- 1 ⟍ of *Peppermint Extract*

Use to .

Physical Development, Health, and Well-Being

CONTENT AREAS

Physical Development, Health, and Well-Being

The Arts

MATERIALS

- Several ribbons, each about 1 foot long
- 3–4 selections of music, preferably in different musical styles
- Music player

17   Ribbon Dancing

Family Messages:

- When children hear music, they seem naturally to want to move to it. Give your child a wide variety of music to listen and move to.

- Moving to music gives your child another way to express himself and practice different ways of moving his body, which promotes physical development and body awareness.

Beginning:

- Give the child a ribbon, and ask him to think of different ways to move it.

- Describe what the child does with the ribbon (say, for example, "You are making it go up and down"), and copy the child's movements.

Middle:

- Play different selections of music, and move with the ribbons.

- When you change songs, ask questions, such as "How does this music sound?" and "How will you move your ribbon to this music?"

- Continue to imitate the child as you move to the different songs.

End:

- Let the child know when the last song is going to be played. Say that when the song ends, it will be time to put the ribbon away.

Home Extensions:

- Encourage parents to think of a time of the day when their child can listen to and move to music at home.

- Help parents think of household objects children can move with while they dance.

18 Batting Balloons

Family Messages:

- As children move in their environment, they develop coordination, improve their physical conditioning, and gain self-confidence about their increasing physical abilities.

Beginning:

- Show the child the balloons and bats, and say "I have brought these things today. What do you think we can do with them?"

- Suggest going outside if possible.

Middle:

- Watch and copy the way the child uses the materials.

- Use the bat to hit the balloon in the air.

- Hit the balloon back and forth between you, the child, and other family members.

End:

- Tell the child that it is time for you to leave.

- Encourage the child to help you put the materials away by batting the balloon toward your belongings.

Home Extensions:

- With parents, think of other lightweight items for their child to toss, kick, or bat, such as beach balls, scarves, rolled socks, and other items to use as bats (see the Materials list).

CONTENT AREAS
Physical Development, Health, and Well-Being

MATERIALS
- 9-inch balloons (*Note:* If popped balloons might be a choking hazard in the home, use large beach balls.)
- Foam bats (or use rolled newspaper, paper plates attached to sticks, or paper towel tubes as bats)

Hitting a ball with a bat helps children develop their hand-eye coordination.

19 Animal Moves

Family Messages:

- Children are physically active. They are able to create movements to imitate their favorite animals (Laney, for example, likes to stretch just like Angel, her cat).

- As children move like their favorite animals, comment on and label their actions. You might say, "Laney, it looks like you are stretching just like Angel does after a nap in the doorway."

- Children often enjoy movement challenges.

Beginning:

- Tell the child that you are thinking of an animal. Ask her to think of an animal too.

- Move like the animal you are thinking of and walk around the room. Ask the child to move around the room like the animal she is thinking of.

- Tell the child that you are thinking of another animal and then move like that second animal. Ask the child to also think of and move like another animal. Repeat this with a third animal/animal movement.

- Have the child assist you in setting up the broom or mop handle between the seats of two chairs.

Middle:

- Say "Let's see if we can move like our favorite animal and go under the broom handle."

- Move like your favorite animal, and try to go *under* the broom handle. Ask the child to move like her favorite animal and try to go *under* the broom handle.

- After three rounds, see if you can move like your favorite animal and go *over* the broom handle. (If the child is not tall enough to go over the broom handle between the two chairs, place it on the floor between the two chairs.)

CONTENT AREAS
Physical Development, Health, and Well-Being

MATERIALS

- 2 chairs
- Mop handle or broom

- Ask the child what other animal movements she could create to go under or over the broom handle. Try out some of these actions.

End:

- Have the child assist in putting away the broom handle and chairs.

- Make a note about the child's suggestions for movements under and over the broom handle to use in the classroom.

Home Extensions:

- Encourage parents to play this game outdoors with their child and to describe the child's actions as she goes over or under the broom handle.

Children love to test their physical abilities, including how fast they can run down a hill!

CONTENT AREAS
Physical Development,
Health, and Well-Being

MATERIALS

- Ball of string or skein
  of yarn

*Families can do this activity
in an open space in their
home with string or rope.*

20 Following the String

Family Messages:

- Children enjoy moving their bodies; they roll, crawl, run,
  gallop, jump, hop, and skip.

- Physical movement builds coordination. As your child
  becomes adept at balance and coordination, her self-
  confidence grows.

Beginning:

- Take the child and family with your ball of string out in the
  yard. If no yard is available, take the child to the park, or get
  permission to do the activity inside.

- Tie the string to the bottom of a tree trunk (or chair). Run
  the string along the ground to other obstacles in the yard
  (for example, unwind more of the string across the lawn and
  under the picnic table and along the ground and over the
  sidewalk). If you are inside, unwind the string under a table,
  across the carpet, and over a chair.

Middle:

- Ask the child to lead you through the obstacle course that
  you have made.

- Move through the obstacle course several times in different
  ways with the child (for example, run, crawl, and hop along
  the string).

End:

- Let the child help you collect the string and roll it back up in
  the ball.

Home Extensions:

- Ask the family members to brainstorm some other ways to
  make an obstacle course in their yard or nearby in a park, or
  even in an open space in their home.

Mathematics

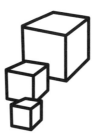

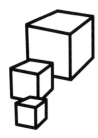

CONTENT AREAS

Mathematics

Social Studies

MATERIALS

- Paper
- Markers
- Pictures of fruits

21   Graphing Favorite Fruits

Family Messages:

- Young children are developing what mathematicians call number sense. They are beginning to understand that numerals represent numbers of objects and are recognizing what has more or less, is bigger or smaller, and so on. Young children are also beginning to estimate and calculate differences in quantity.

- Children also know that others have different tastes and interests.

Beginning:

- Lay out the pictures of fruit.

- Talk about which is your favorite fruit.

- Ask the child which is his favorite. For instance, you might ask, "Why is it your favorite?" Draw out the child's reasons with open-ended questions and comments. For example, the child might like the fruit's color, texture, or taste, or just that it goes well with ice cream.

Middle:

- Make a graph using your favorite fruit and the child's as a beginning (see the sample graph on the next page).

- Ask what family members are present to choose their favorite fruit and put it on the graph.

- Ask the child "Which fruit seems to be the favorite? Which fruits are left out?"

End:

- Put the graph on the refrigerator so other family members can weigh in as they come home.

Home Extensions:

- What other things can the family think of that they could make a graph with? Favorite cookies? Favorite sports? Food they don't like?

- Ask the child to bring the fruit graph back to school.

Our Favorite Fruit

Ms. Kay	🍌	
DeShawn	🍎	

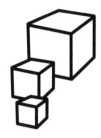

CONTENT AREAS
Mathematics

MATERIALS

- 10 small people or animal figures
- Scarf or other long piece of fabric

22   Ten in the Bed

Family Messages:

- Rote counting is saying numbers in order by memory. This is one aspect of learning to count.

- Children also need to manipulate small numbers of real objects (touch, handle, move, sort, and group them) to develop an understanding of what the numbers mean.

- Children develop an understanding of how numbers work by solving different types of number problems as they work directly with real objects.

Beginning:

- Lay the scarf out on a table, and place the figures on top.

- Explain to the child that the scarf is a bed and the figures are sleeping.

- Ask "How many are sleeping in the bed?"

Middle:

- Sing "Ten in the Bed" with the child, beginning with "There were 10 (or other number) in the bed and the little one said…"

- Ask the child to make one of the figures roll off the bed.

- Repeat the song or chant a few times. Ask the child to say whether one, two, or three figures should roll off.

- Ask the child to predict how many figures will be left on the bed.

End:

- When all the figures are off the bed, ask the child to help you count them as you put them away.

Home Extensions:

- Ask the child and parents to think of objects at home that could be used to reenact the story again (such as a dish towel and spoons).

23 Looking for Numbers

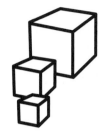

Family Messages:

- Just as we want children to learn the ABCs, we also want them to learn numerals.

- You can help your child learn numerals by calling attention to them in the environment and showing your child how they are useful in our lives.

Beginning:

- Display the items you have brought and identify the numbers with the child's help.

- Ask the child to think of other things that have numbers on them.

Middle:

- Look around the room or house for objects with numbers.

- Encourage the child to point to and name the numbers.

- Point out and name unknown numbers.

End:

- Tell the child that it is time for you to leave. Ask him to walk you to the door.

- With the child, look for the house address or apartment number near the door.

Home Extensions:

- Ask parents to call attention to numbers throughout their environment. Some examples include numbered grocery store aisles, gas station signs, highway exit signs, and elevator buttons.

CONTENT AREAS
Mathematics

MATERIALS

- Selection of objects that have numbers on them (for example, phone, calculator, numbered race car)

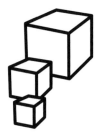

CONTENT AREAS
Mathematics

MATERIALS

- 3–4 pictures of familiar objects, such as animals from old calendars and magazines
- Cardboard or cardstock
- Clear contact paper for laminating

24   Picture Puzzles

Family Messages:

- Putting puzzles together helps children develop spatial reasoning, which is a component of geometry and an important aspect of mechanical skills.

- Children have to have an idea of what an object looks like (picture it in their minds) in order to piece it back together.

Beginning:

- Tell the child that you have some homemade puzzles to use today.

- Hand the child a piece of one of the puzzles, and ask her to guess what she thinks the picture might be. Ask "How do you know that?"

Middle:

- Encourage the child to piece the puzzle together.

- Use direction words, such as *turn* and *flip,* and position words, such as *above, next to,* and *underneath.*

End:

- When the puzzle is complete, talk about whether the child's initial guess about the picture was correct.

Home Extensions:

- Suggest that parents make (or help their child make) puzzles out of the fronts of cereal or cracker boxes.

How to Make a Puzzle

- Attach the picture to cardboard or cardstock.
- Cut out the picture into 4–10 pieces (depending on the developmental level of the child).
- Cover each piece with clear contact paper (or laminate) to make sturdier puzzle pieces.

25 Play Dough and Marbles

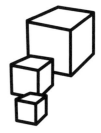

Family Messages:

- Rote counting is saying numbers in order by memory, one aspect of learning to count.

- Children learn to understand what numbers mean by touching and moving real objects.

- Children often judge quantity based on appearance.

Beginning:

- Pass out one play dough portion to the child and to every person there (save one portion for you). Say something like "I have special play dough today. See if you can find out what makes it special."

- Acknowledge the child's discovery of the hidden objects.

Middle:

- Make a general comment about the quantity of objects discovered. For example, you might say, "You are finding many marbles" or "That looks like a lot of marbles."

- Remove the objects from your own play dough and line them up in front of you. Say something like "I have a lot too. I wonder how many?" (The child may start counting his marbles or your marbles either by rote or with one-to-one correspondence.)

- Model counting your marbles, comparing quantities, or making sets of different amounts based on the developmental level of the child.

End:

- Have the child help you remove all the marbles from the play dough and put the materials away.

CONTENT AREAS
Mathematics

MATERIALS

- Play dough portions (one for each participant) with marbles, stones, or other small objects hidden inside

Home Extensions:

- Find fun and unusual things to count, such as freckles on an arm, buttons on a shirt, or steps it takes to go from one place to another.

- Encourage parents to count objects as part of their daily life (for example, the number of forks needed to set the table or the number of people in line at the grocery store).

Encourage parents to have their children count, as this child and her mother are counting together the days until her birthday.

26 Measuring by Leaps and Bounds

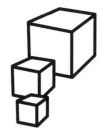

Family Messages:

- This activity will give your child practice estimating, measuring, and counting with nonstandard units of measure (for example, hands, feet, shoes).

Beginning:

- Say something like "Let's guess how many hops to the garage (or wall or fence)."

- Then ask "What else could we measure with different kinds of steps (giant, baby, hops, leaps)?"

Middle:

- On the paper, let the child record, or help the child to record, her estimate of how many _____ to the

  _____.

- Let the child measure with steps, hops, leaps, or lengths of her arm.

- Record the child's answer next to the guess.

End:

- Look at the results of what the child estimated and what was actually measured.

- Ask "What did we learn?"

Home Extensions:

- Let children use a hand or foot to measure in addition to using a yardstick.

- Encourage parents to try out new ideas for measuring. For instance, a parent might say, "How many of Dad's feet will it take to get from the car to the front door?"

CONTENT AREAS
Mathematics

Physical Development and Health

MATERIALS
- Paper
- Pencils
- Yardstick

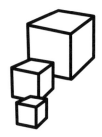

CONTENT AREAS

Mathematics

Science and Technology

MATERIALS

- Large circle, triangle, or rectangle cut out of cardstock or other sturdy material (choose one shape per visit)
- Paper and pencil

27   Shape Hunt

Family Messages:

- Children are keen observers.

- Children organize information into categories based on specific characteristics (such as shape).

- Recognizing shapes is an element of geometry.

Beginning:

- Show the child the large shape you have brought with you.

- Name the shape and talk about its features. You might, for example, talk about how a circle is curved, has no points or corners, and is round like a ball.

Middle:

- Look around the room or house for other items of that shape.

- When developmentally appropriate, you might, with the child, compile a list of the items you see in the room or house that matches the shape you brought with you.

End:

- Give the child the cut-out shape to keep.

- Look for more objects of that shape as you and the child walk to the door.

Home Extensions:

- Encourage families to look for shapes in other environments, such as outdoors or at the store.

Science and Technology

CONTENT AREAS
Science and Technology

MATERIALS

- Cloth tote bag (or any opaque bag)
- Small toys from the classroom, which are familiar to the child

28   It's in the Bag

Family Messages:

- Children use all their senses to explore and learn about the physical world.

- Children must remember the features of familiar objects (by forming images in their brains) and compare those memories to the objects they are touching.

Beginning:

- Place the toys out on a table and, with the child, identify each toy.

- Remove the toys from the table.

- Have the child close her eyes while you place one of the toys into the bag.

Middle:

- Ask the child to put her hand into the bag and feel the toy inside.

- Ask her to describe what she feels and guess which toy it is.

- Ask "How did you know it was that toy?"

End:

- Take turns describing features of each toy as you put them away. Say, for example, "I'm putting away the toy with four wheels."

Home Extensions:

- Encourage parents to look for opportunities to describe objects for their child to guess. For example, when they are at the grocery store with their child, they might say, "We need some fruit that is long and has a yellow peel."

29 Magnets

Family Messages:

- Children are natural scientists, observing and investigating what things are made of and how things work.

- Part of "doing" science is predicting and then testing ideas to discover the properties of objects and how objects can interact with one another.

Beginning:

- Introduce the magnet and explain that it attracts some objects that are made of metal.

- Place the assortment of materials on the table, and say "Some of these things will stick to a magnet. How can we find out which ones are magnetic?"

Middle:

- Use the magnets to determine which objects are magnetic (not all things made of metal are magnetic).

- Ask the child to predict whether an object is magnetic. Ask "How do you know?" to learn more about the child's thinking.

End:

- Before putting the magnets away, ask the child to look around the room for two other objects he thinks are magnetic. (Be sure child does not put a magnet on a computer or television screen.)

Home Extensions:

- Encourage parents to talk with their child about what objects are made of (for example, wood, plastic, metal, cloth).

- Suggest that families play I spy, and give clues about the properties of an object (for example, "I spy something that is red and made of wood").

CONTENT AREAS
Science and Technology

MATERIALS
- Magnet wands or other large magnets
- Assorted materials (magnetic and nonmagnetic)

CONTENT AREAS
Science and Technology

MATERIALS

- 6 plastic water bottles filled with different items (for example, salt, sand, dried beans or rice, buttons, nuts and bolts) to make different sounds when shaken

- Bandana or cloth for a blindfold

30 Listening to Shakers

Family Messages:

- Children need opportunities to use all their senses to learn about the world.

- When we ask children to pay attention to sounds in the environment, they sharpen their sense of sound.

Beginning:

- Show the child the water bottles, and talk about how each sounds different when shaken.

Middle:

- Blindfold the child (or ask the child to close her eyes) while you shake one of the bottles.

- Ask the child to guess which bottle you shook. Ask "How did you know?"

- Switch roles — have the child shake a bottle while you are blindfolded.

End:

- Ask the child to help you put the bottles away.

Home Extensions:

- Encourage parents to make a shaker with their child. Suggest that they use pebbles, buttons, or coins.

- Encourage parents to take a "sound walk" with their child to listen to sounds in the neighborhood.

31   Soapy Suds

Family Messages:

- Science is an active process where children observe the physical world, investigate how things work, test their own ideas, and come to their own conclusions.

- Children need to handle and explore materials to discover the properties of those materials and how certain actions can cause materials to change.

Beginning:

- Pour water into the dish tub so it is no more than 1 inch high.

- Tell the child that you would like to make lots of soap suds. Ask "How do you think we can do that?"

Middle:

- Pour soap onto a sponge, and just place it in the water without swishing it.

- Ask "Now what do we have to do?"

- Squeeze the sponges to make lots of soap suds.

- Encourage the child to describe what he is doing to make the bubbles.

End:

- Have the child help you rinse out the tub and the sponges in the sink.

Home Extensions:

- Suggest that parents might try this activity at bath time.

- Encourage parents to repeat this activity by putting soap onto a washcloth to see if this produces as many bubbles as the soap on the sponge.

CONTENT AREAS
Science and Technology

MATERIALS
- Dish tub
- 2–3 sponges or enough sponges for each person who is participating
- Dishwashing liquid (no-tears formula)
- Water

CONTENT AREAS
Science and Technology

MATERIALS

- 2 sand timers of different sizes
- Tub of small stones, rice, sand, or beads
- 7 paper or plastic cups
- Paper and pencil

Homemade Sand Timer

To make your own sand timer, attach two clear plastic bottles with a Tornado Tube and fill the bottle with sand or salt. (Tornado Tubes can be purchased through teacher supply catalogs.)

---

32   Using Timers

Family Messages:

- Time is an abstract concept for young children; they measure time in concrete and sensory ways. As children form mental images, they are able to remember past events and anticipate future events.

- In this home visit activity, your child will relate lengths of time to an event.

Beginning:

- Bring out the sand timers for the child to explore.

- Ask the child to predict which timer empties faster.

Middle:

- Show the child the tub filled with stones (or other material you have brought). Ask him to predict how many cups he thinks he can fill with stones before the sand has run out of the timer.

- Turn the timer over, and see how close the child comes to his prediction.

- Have the child use the sand timer to time you as you attempt to fill the cups.

- Ask the child and family members for ideas about what else to time. He might say something like, "I can go from the door to the garage before the timer has emptied." See if the child's and/or family members' predictions are correct.

End:

- Make a list of the things that you, the child, and family members were able to time during the visit.

Home Extensions:

- Ask if the family has a kitchen timer or a stopwatch to time events for the child (for example, the child might pick up toys or put on a coat to go outdoors). Ask the family to predict (and have the child predict) how much time it will take to complete the tasks.

33 Noticing Changes in Nature

CONTENT AREAS
Science and Technology

Family Messages:

- The changes that take place in the natural cycles of plants and animals heighten children's awareness of the passage of time and the changes that occur.

Beginning:

- Lay out the photographs of the fruit tree on the table.
- Ask the child which photo is the first thing that happens before fruit can grow on a tree.

Middle:

- Talk about each stage in the tree's cycle. For instance, the photos may show leaves; buds; flowers; small fruit; and, finally, ripe fruit. The photos may also show the tree after the fruit has been harvested, with leaves that change color and fall off.
- Encourage the child to talk about the photos.
- Allow the child to put them in order, if he chooses.
- Go outside, and look at the trees with the child and parents. Talk about the kinds of trees that you see. Ask "Do any of the trees bear fruit?"

End:

- Find a deciduous tree (a tree that sheds off its leaves for part of the year), and take a photo of the family in front of the tree.

Home Extensions:

- Suggest to the family that they look at a family photo album with the child that shows his growth from a baby to a pre-

MATERIALS

- Camera
- 8 photos illustrating the cycle of a fruit tree (or a tree appropriate for your geographic region)

schooler. If the family has raised a pet, they can also show photos of the pet as a puppy or kitten.

- Be sure to take a family picture in front of the tree during each season to notice the changes in the tree (and in the family)!

Let parents know of local fruit orchards so their families can have a hands-on experience (and taste) of the stages in a tree's cycle.

Social Studies

CONTENT AREAS
Social Studies

The Arts

MATERIALS

- Blanket or flat sheet
- Paper plates, cups, and napkins
- Thermos and/or other items used on picnics
- Picnic basket or bag for carrying materials
- Dress-up items, such as hats or dolls

34   Going on a Picnic

Family Messages:

- When children pretend, they imitate what they understand about the world and use their imaginations to express fantasies.

- Watching your child's pretend play gives you an opportunity to see how your child pictures the world.

- You can support your child's pretend play by imitating what your child is doing and letting your child be the leader of the play.

Beginning:

- Ask the child if he has ever been on a picnic, and if so, what he remembers about it.

- Explain that you would like to go on a picnic inside the house.

Middle:

- Ask the child to help you figure out a good place to spread out the blanket.

- Invite the child to join you on the blanket for the picnic and to look through the basket with you.

- Ask the child what he would like to eat and drink.

- Continue the picnic, following the child's ideas about how the picnic should progress.

End:

- Say that you must finish eating because it is getting late (or dark or because it looks like rain).

- Pack up the picnic, and pretend to go home.

Home Extensions:

- Encourage parents to plan another pretend picnic or plan to eat a snack or meal outside on a blanket with their child.

35   Singing Songs

Family Messages:

- Children enjoy exploring the wide range of sounds they can make with their voices, including humming and singing.

- Sing along with your child to encourage his singing, and listen to a variety of musical styles.

Beginning:

- Show the child the song cards, and see which songs he remembers from preschool.

Middle:

- Have the child choose several songs, and sing one together. Tap a steady beat on your legs before you begin singing.

- Ask the child if he knows another song that is not on the song card. Encourage him to sing it for you.

End:

- Make up a song to let the child know it is time for you to leave (use a familiar tune or make up your own tune). For example, sing the following to the tune of "Here We Go Round the Mulberry Bush":

    Now it's time for me to go
    Me to go
    Me to go
    Now it's time for me to go
    I'll see you at preschool (or next time I come).

Home Extensions:

- Leave some blank cards so parents can help their child make song cards at home.

- Ask parents to think of different times of the day when they can use the song cards (for example, at bedtime, in the car).

CONTENT AREAS
Social Studies

The Arts

MATERIALS

- Song cards, each with the name of a familiar song and a simple picture or symbol to represent the song

- Blank cards to leave with parents for Home Extensions

A song book provides a visual reminder of the children's favorite songs in pictures and words.

CONTENT AREAS
Social Studies

The Arts

MATERIALS

- Baby doll
- Blanket
- Blank paper book

36 Babysitting

Family Messages:

- Young children are developing skills to look at things from another person's point of view. They are also developing empathy.

- Giving children experiences in which they have opportunities to understand and practice caring for others leads to feelings of empathy.

Beginning:

- Ask the child what he knows about babies. Ask "What do babies need?"

- Give the child the baby doll.

Middle:

- Talk about the child's suggestions.

- See if there are items in the child's home that the child has suggested that a baby might need, such as a baby blanket or a small spoon for feeding.

- Let the child lead in caring for the baby.

End:

- Sing a lullaby, such as "Rock-a-Bye Baby."

- Find a baby doll at home for the child to babysit.

- Tell the child that there is a blank book to fill in with the family about how the child "babysat" for the baby.

Home Extensions:

- Encourage the parents to write down how the child cared for the baby. Suggest that they ask the child some or all of the following: "What did the baby eat?" "Where did the baby sleep?" "How did you play with the baby?"

The Arts

CONTENT AREAS
The Arts

MATERIALS
- Watercolors
- Paintbrushes
- Cup with water
- Paper
- Newspaper to cover work surface
- Smocks

37   Painting With Watercolors

Family Messages:

- Children need time to explore materials (such as paint) before they can actually paint something recognizable.

- In the exploration stage, children are more interested in the process of using the paint and less concerned about how their final picture looks.

- As children become more familiar with art materials, they gradually move from accidental discovery (such as making a line and deciding it looks like a snake) to intentional representations.

Beginning:

- Introduce the watercolor pallet, and explore with the child what happens when you add water to the paint.

- Imitate the child as she explores paint and water on paper.

Middle:

- Listen to the child describe her work. Make comments about what you see the child doing, such as "You're rubbing your paintbrush around and around in the paint."

- Use your paintbrush in different ways to create different types of lines. Describe your own actions and the lines you make. For example, you might brush up and down very fast and call your lines *zigzags*.

End:

- Say one thing you like about painting as you put away your materials.

- Ask the child if she would like to display her picture in the house. With parents, decide where the picture should be displayed.

Home Extensions:

- Suggest that the child use paintbrushes with soap in the bathtub or use paintbrushes with plain water on the sidewalk.

Before children make intentional representations, they need time to explore the materials used for painting.

CONTENT AREAS
The Arts

MATERIALS
• Crayons
• Plain paper

38 Drawing With Crayons

Family Messages:

• Give your child plain paper to draw on.

• Early representations consist of simple forms that gradually become more detailed.

• Encourage your child to do her own artwork and describe what she has drawn. Avoid making models for your child to copy.

Beginning:

• Set out the paper and crayons. Point out to the child that the paper is plain, so she can use her imagination to make different types of marks, shapes, or other representations.

Middle:

• Observe the way the child draws on the paper.

• Imitate the types of lines or shapes she makes, and describe what you are doing. For example, you might say, "I'm making fast lines that go up and down, just like you are making."

• If the child is making a detailed representation, help her think about other details to add, such as straight or curly hair on a person, apples on a tree, or a door or windows on a house.

• Make and describe other types of lines or shapes, such as wavy, thick, or curved lines; circles; or triangles. Use words to compare lines and shapes, such as *large* and *small, dark* and *light,* and *squiggly* and *straight.*

End:

• When the child finishes coloring, say "Tell me about your picture."

• Accept the child's description or explanation. For example, a child may call a page full of colorful squiggles a dinosaur. You might say, "Yes, you used lots of squiggly lines to make a dinosaur."

- Ask the child if she would like to display her picture in the house. With her parents, decide where the picture should be displayed.

Home Extensions:

- Leave several sheets of blank paper with the family.

- Ask the child to draw a picture at home that she can bring to school and put in a class book or to keep at home to show you at your next home visit.

If the child has a hard time coming up with something to draw, suggest that he draw something that he did that day, like this child did — a picture of his teacher coming for a home visit!

CONTENT AREAS
The Arts

Language, Literacy, and Communication

MATERIALS

- Postcards of paintings, such as Mary Cassatt's *The Boating Party,* Claude Monet's *The Artist's Garden at Vetheuil,* and Pierre-Auguste Renoir's *A Girl With a Watering Can*

- 3 different kinds of paper (for example, newsprint, manila paper, or drawing paper)

- Chalk

- Pencils

- Old newspapers for protecting a surface during drawing (*Note:* This activity can be done outdoors, just as many artists paint.)

39 Art Appreciation

Family Messages:

- The arts play an important role in cognitive, motor, language, and social-emotional development. As children engage in the artistic process, they learn to observe, organize, and interpret experiences.

- Your child's representations will develop from simple to complex; her representations grow from her real experiences. Every child's representations are unique.

- Children are able to appreciate as well as make art.

Beginning:

- Lay out the postcards, and let the child look at, touch, and talk about the ones she likes.

- Talk about what she sees. Ask "What do you think is happening in the picture?" Talk about colors and textures.

Middle:

- Let the child choose paper, chalk, and pencils.

- Be sure to use the materials yourself. Imitate what the child does with the materials.

- Talk about textures and colors in the child's work. Let the child take the lead.

End:

- Finish the activity by finding a place to display the artwork with the parents' help.

- Let the child assist with packing up the materials.

Home Extensions:

- Ask the family where they might be able to display their child's works of art.

- Ask the family if they can find a place for the child to keep things such as crayons, markers, paints, and paper for drawing and painting at home.

- Discuss the possibilities for things to use as paper to draw on — newspapers, paper towels, and old magazines often work well. Suggest using Q-Tips for painting too.

Young children are capable of appreciating as well as making art.

CONTENT AREAS
The Arts

Science and Technology

MATERIALS

- Heavyweight paper
- Glue
- Variety of collage materials with different textures (for example, cotton, sand paper, fabric pieces, feathers, aluminum foil)

40   Texture Collage

Family Messages:

- Classification means grouping or organizing things by a common trait.

- Children use all their senses to sort objects by different properties.

- Children classify things to help them organize their understanding of the world.

Beginning:

- Introduce the collage materials, and encourage the child to describe them. Model descriptive words, such as *soft*, *shiny*, or *bumpy*.

Middle:

- Use paper and glue to create a collage with the materials, and encourage the child to create a collage as well.

- As you are working, continue to describe materials. For example, you might say, "I'm choosing soft things."

- Encourage the child to think of other things in her house that are similar to the materials you have brought. You might say, "This aluminum foil is shiny, and the kitchen faucet is shiny."

End:

- Ask the child to help you put away unused materials.

- Talk with the child about her collage. Say something like "Let's look at your collage together. Tell me what you did."

Home Extensions:

- Go on a treasure hunt around the house. Find items with similar attributes (for example, things that are soft, shiny, or made of wood).

About the Authors

Suzanne Gainsley is a HighScope certified trainer and teacher who has been teaching at the HighScope Demonstration Preschool since 1998. She has also worked with infants, toddlers, preschoolers, and elementary school children in various settings as a teacher, parent, and volunteer. Gainsley is the author of *From Message to Meaning: Using a Daily Message Board in the Preschool Classroom;* coauthor of two books in the Teacher's Idea Book Series (from HighScope Press), *"I'm Older Than You. I'm Five!" Math in the Preschool Classroom* and *50 Large-Group Activities for Active Learners;* and a contributing writer for *Small-Group Times to Scaffold Early Learning,* also in the Teacher's Idea Book Series.

Julie Hoelscher is an Early Childhood Specialist at the HighScope Educational Research Foundation. She has been an infant/toddler caregiver, preschool teacher, early childhood center director, resource counselor, teacher trainer, and an elementary school reform coach. Hoelscher also writes articles on classroom teaching practices for HighScope's *Extensions.*